WATER POWER

IAN GRAHAM

WAYLAND

ENERGY FOREVER?

Water Power

OTHER TITLES IN THE SERIES

Solar Power · Wind Power · Fossil Fuels
Nuclear Power · Geothermal and Bioenergy

Produced for Wayland Publishers Ltd by
Lionheart Books, 10 Chelmsford Square, London NW10 3AR

Designer: Ben White
Editor: Lionel Bender
Picture Research: Madeleine Samuel
Electronic make-up: Mike Pilley, Radius/Pelican Graphics
Illustrated by Rudi Vizi

First published in 1998 by Wayland Publishers Ltd
61 Western Road, Hove, East Sussex BN3 1JD

Find Wayland on the internet at http://www.wayland.co.uk

British Library Cataloguing in Publication Data
Graham, Ian, 1953-
Water power. - (Energy Forever?)
1. Water-power - Juvenile literature
I. Title
333.9'14

ISBN 0 7502 2103 8

Printed and bound by G. Canale & C.S.p.A., Turin

Picture Acknowledgements
Cover: Tony Stone/Getty Images/Tom Bean. Stockmarket: title page, 9,
20-21 (Ballantyne), 25 (Rose). US Department of Energy: pages 4-5. Ole
Steen Hansen, Denmark: page 5. Lionheart Books: pages 6-7. Eye
Ubiquitous: pages 7 (NASA), title page, 16-17 (Brian Pickering), 41 (Steve
Lindridge), 43 (Davy Bold). Ecoscene: pages 8-9 (Andrew Brown), 10
(Chris Knapton), 12-13 (Erik Shaffer), 13 (Andrew Brown), 14-15 (Richard
Glover), 26 (Joan Creed), 32 (Rob Nichol), 36 (Nick Hawkes), 40 (M.
Jones). Mary Evans Picture Library: pages 17, 19 (both), 20. AEA
Technology: pages 22, 30, 30-31, 31, 34, 38-39. Samfoto: pages 28-29
(Jon Arne Sieter), 29 (Morten Loberg). Kvaernar Brug, Norway: page 32
(both). Bruce Coleman Ltd (Gordon Langsbury) page 35. Frank Lane
Picture Agency/ McCutcheon, Alaska, USA: pages 42-43.

CONTENTS

WHAT IS WATER POWER?

Introduction

Water power is the use of water to do work, such as producing electricity or driving mills. Water power is kinder to the environment than burning fossil fuels, in particular coal, oil and gas, because it produces no air pollution or poisonous waste. Water is also a renewable resource – it can be used again and again.

A view of water gushing through the John Day Dam on the Washington-Oregon State border in the USA. It is one of several dams on the Columbia River that together provide more than 22,000 megawatts of electrical power to the Pacific northwest region of America.

Water powered machines have been used for thousands of years, but water power declined when cheap fossil fuels became more popular during the first half of the twentieth century. Steep increases in oil prices in the 1970s, and greater concern about pollution, has made water power more attractive once again.

Energy from running water is free. And it can be turned into useful work quite easily. While many water power projects use expensive new technology to make them as big and efficient as possible, simple hand-made wooden machines can make use of water power, too. This book explores the history, the technology, the environmental impact and the future of water power.

Above: Water cascades over the water wheels at this Danish water mill. The mill is used to grind grain to make flour. Few water mills survive today, but once thousands of them lined the banks of rivers across Europe.

Above: The vast power potential of Niagara Falls on the US-Canadian border was tapped first in 1757. Hydroelectric power stations at the Falls now produce a flow of more than 4,000 megawatts of electricity – enough to supply the needs of a large city.

Water heated by the Sun evaporates and rises into the atmosphere. Winds carry it to regions of cooler air where it condenses into water droplets, which fall as rain. The water flows down to rivers, lakes and the sea, and the cycle begins again.

Where does water come from?

Water covers nearly three-quarters of the Earth's surface, but it was not always like this. When our planet was forming 4.6 billion years ago, water did not exist because it was so hot. As the Earth cooled, atoms of hydrogen and oxygen gases linked together to form water molecules. Vast clouds of water vapour swirled around the planet.

When the Earth cooled enough for the vapour to condense into water droplets, scientists believe that it may have rained all over the Earth for hundreds of years! So much rain fell that the lowest parts of the planet filled up with water to form the oceans. But the water did not stay there. Ever since those distant prehistoric times water has constantly moved around the Earth in the clouds, rain, rivers and oceans.

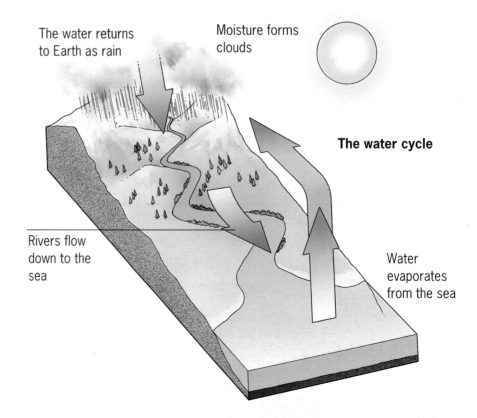

The water returns to Earth as rain

Moisture forms clouds

The water cycle

Rivers flow down to the sea

Water evaporates from the sea

FACTFILE

Plants move vast quantities of water from the ground to the atmosphere. Water is drawn up into a plant through its roots. The water leaves the plant again by evaporating from microscopic holes in its leaves. A single oak tree can move 400 litres of water from the ground to the atmosphere in a day.

The Earth is unique among the nine planets of the solar system. It is the only planet where water exists in its liquid form, with deep oceans as well as an oxygen-rich atmosphere with water vapour clouds.

Why is water so important?

Water is essential for life. The driest places on Earth are the places where there is the least life – the fewest plants and animals. The first forms of life on Earth developed in the sea. When plants and animals spread from the sea on to land, they continued to need water to survive. Green plants combine water and simple chemicals from the soil with carbon dioxide from the atmosphere to make food. Green plants are important because almost every other creature eats either plants or other creatures that themselves eat plants.

Plants grow only where they find water. In Israel's Negev Desert, plants grow along the edge of a seasonal stream. In places where underground water comes to the surface, green oases are formed.

More than half of the weight of a human being is water. We constantly lose water as perspiration, moisture in our breath, and when we go to the toilet. So we each have to replace about 2.5 litres of fresh water every day. We drink about a litre and the rest comes from our food. We can do without food for several weeks, but we can only survive for a few days without fresh water.

Water is also needed for washing, watering plants and by industry. Only 1per cent of all our water is freely available fresh water. 97 per cent is salty water in the sea and the remaining 2 per cent is fresh water locked up in glaciers, underground and in polar ice caps.

In nature, water always flows downhill under the force of gravity. If it is to be sent uphill or sprayed out of a hose, then it has to be pumped under pressure.

What causes the tides?

The sea level rises and falls about once every 12 hours. These daily changes in depth are known as the tides. The tides, which range from high to low sea levels and back again, are mainly caused by our closest neighbour in space, the Moon. The Moon is so close to us – only 400,000 kilometres away – that its gravity pulls strongly on the Earth. It pulls water towards the side of the Earth that is closest to it, causing high tides there.

Each day the tides are later than on the day before because the Moon rises later each day. As it circles the spinning Earth, the Moon climbs above the horizon (the imaginary horizontal line between the sea and sky) about 50 minutes later every day, and the tides follow it. The Sun affects the tides, too. The height of the tides depends on the positions of the Sun, Moon and Earth. The highest tides, called spring tides, occur at the Full Moon and New Moon when the Earth, Moon and Sun all line up together.

FACTFILE

The movement of huge quantities of water round the Earth by the Moon as the tides come in (high tide) and go out (low tide) affects shipping. The captains of ships have to be sure when sea levels are deep enough for them to sail into ports or to follow certain sea routes. In some places, high tide can be 5 metres above low tide.

Here, as the Sun sets, the Moon rises over the Mediterranean island of Corsica. The changing positions of the Earth and these two heavenly bodies are responsible for the daily rise and fall of tides around our coasts.

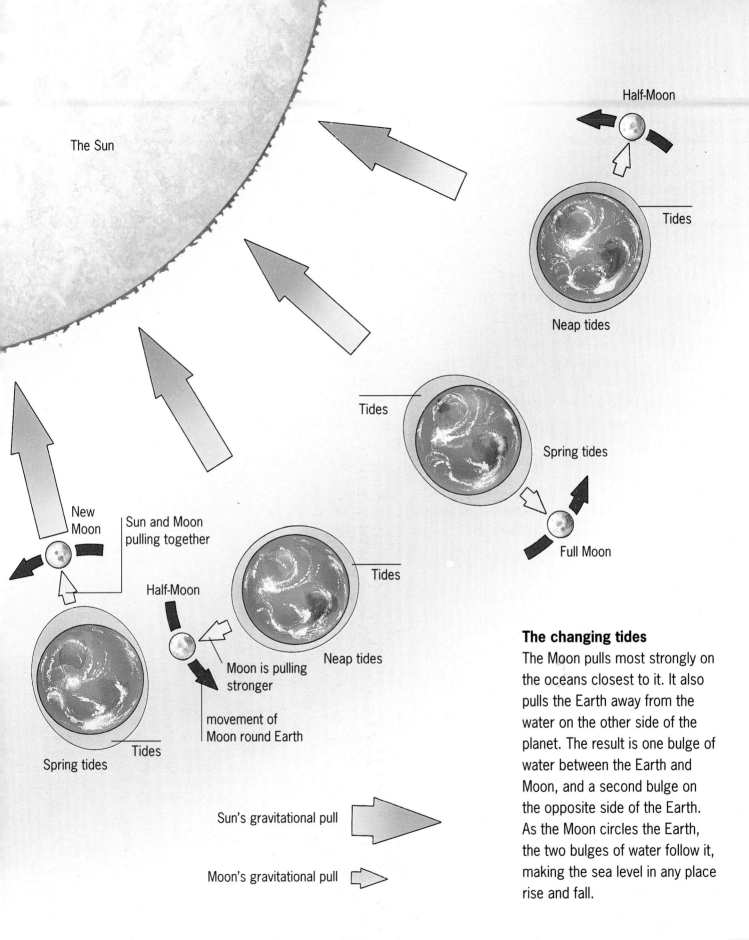

The Sun

Half-Moon

Tides

Neap tides

Tides

Spring tides

Full Moon

New Moon

Sun and Moon pulling together

Half-Moon

Tides

Neap tides

Moon is pulling stronger

movement of Moon round Earth

Tides

Spring tides

Sun's gravitational pull

Moon's gravitational pull

The changing tides
The Moon pulls most strongly on the oceans closest to it. It also pulls the Earth away from the water on the other side of the planet. The result is one bulge of water between the Earth and Moon, and a second bulge on the opposite side of the Earth. As the Moon circles the Earth, the two bulges of water follow it, making the sea level in any place rise and fall.

The power of water in nature

The world's coastlines are constantly battered by the sea. Waves churn up the seashore. Depending on the currents, tides and winds, the waves wash material away from some places and deposit it somewhere else. The constant removal of material from parts of the coast, called coastal erosion, can make cliffs collapse and cause whole villages to fall into the sea.

The highest tides may overwhelm sea defences and flood vast areas of land, causing great loss of life in some places. The western half of the Netherlands is below sea level. The Dutch people famously protected their country by building land barriers called dykes. In 1953, high tides broke through the dykes and flooded the countryside, killing 1,800 people.

Floods are not always destructive. In ancient Egypt, farmers depended on the River Nile flooding to carry rich river mud on to their land and feed their crops. Ice can change the landscape in dramatic ways, too. Glaciers carve out deep U-shaped valleys as they slowly flow down to the sea over many centuries.

F A C T F I L E

Earthquakes under the sea can produce massive waves called tsunami. In 1868, an earthquake in the Pacific Ocean produced a tsunami that surged to a height of 14 m as it hit the coast of Chile. It was so powerful that it carried an American warship 3 km inland. About 25,000 people died in the flood caused by this tsunami.

A house collapses into the sea in County Wexford, Ireland, as the constant pounding of waves eat away the cliffs below it.

Inset photo opposite Atlantic waves have carved their way through these shale cliffs on the coast of Cornwall, England, leaving solitary pillars of rock.

A torrential downpour drenches a tropical beach. Air heavily laden with moisture from the oceans rises over the hot land. As the air rises, its temperature falls. Cool air cannot hold as much moisture as warm air. Eventually, the moisture falls to the land as rain.

FACTFILE

Every year between about April and October, winds blowing across India from the north-east reverse direction. Instead of blowing across the dry Asian land mass, they blow over the Indian Ocean before they reach India. They collect moisture from the ocean and release it as heavy rain on India. Winds that change direction with the seasons like this are called monsoon winds.

How do the oceans affect weather?

The world's oceans have a major effect on our weather and long-term climate. They store some of the Sun's heat and spread it around the Earth.

Within the oceans there are distinct and generally horizontal flows of sea water in various directions. These ocean currents are caused by a combination of wind currents in the atmosphere, tidal motion and the emptying of rivers along coasts. There are also vertical flows of sea water caused by warm water, being less dense than cold water, rising to the surface. There it gives up some of its heat to the air, cools, then sinks back down.

Similarly, as air above the sea warms, it rises. As it does so, it cools, becomes heavier and sinks back down. Moisture evaporating from the sea is carried upwards in the warm air, then condenses to form clouds and eventually falls as rain. This creates the weather cycle.

Ocean Conveyor Belt
The main ocean current, the Great Ocean Conveyor Belt, stretches all round the world and from pole to pole. Deep cold water near the South Pole flows into the warmer Indian and Pacific Oceans. As the water warms, it rises and flows west into the Atlantic Ocean. The water then turns north, cools, sinks again and flows towards the South Pole.

 Warm-water currents

Cold-water currents

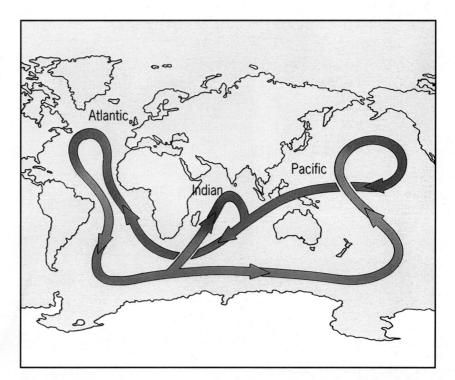

WATER POWER IN HISTORY

Water wheels

Water was the main source of power for industry for 4,000 years. The first machine built to take advantage of water power was the water wheel. A water wheel is a wheel with paddles fixed round its rim. When the wheel is dipped in moving water, the force of water pushing against the paddles turns it. The axle, through the centre of the wheel, can be connected to a heavy millstone, to grind grain.

The Ancient Egyptians were probably the first to use water wheels, on the River Nile, as early as 2,000 BC.

FACTFILE

Water power spread rapidly in Medieval times, between about the tenth and fifteenth centuries. The Domesday Book, a survey of England written in 1086, records 5,624 water mills. Water-powered grain mills were common throughout Europe and the Middle East by the third century. By the sixth century, European cities had grown to such a size that it was impossible to feed their people without the use of water power.

A water wheel on the River Test in England. Most water-powered mills and machines disappeared during the nineteenth century as steam engines took over from water power. Most of the water wheels were dismantled or left to decay, but a few mills with working water wheels have survived to the present day.

Right: This sixteenth-century French water wheel operated a series of bellows to force air into furnaces. A complicated series of mechanical links converted the spinning motion of the wheel into a rocking motion that pumped the handles of the bellows up and down.

But the first clear description of a water wheel was written by the Roman architect Vitruvius in 27 BC. According to Vitruvius, the water wheel was in everyday use by then, having been invented by Greek engineers. The Greek geographer Strabo described seeing a water-powered wheel called the hydraletes in 24 BC at Cabeira in the Pontus, in present-day Turkey. Most of these early water wheels drove millstones to make flour, but they were known to have been used for other purposes too. Some of them operated hammers or bellows in iron forges.

The power of the tides

In places where rivers flowed too slowly to turn a water wheel, Medieval engineers discovered that they could use the rise and fall of the tides as a source of energy. The incoming tide flowed too slowly to be of use, but the water could be stored for use later. The rising waters of the incoming tide were trapped behind wooden gates. As the tide turned, it pushed the gates closed, trapping the water behind them. When the tide had retreated, the water was allowed to flow through the mill wheel.

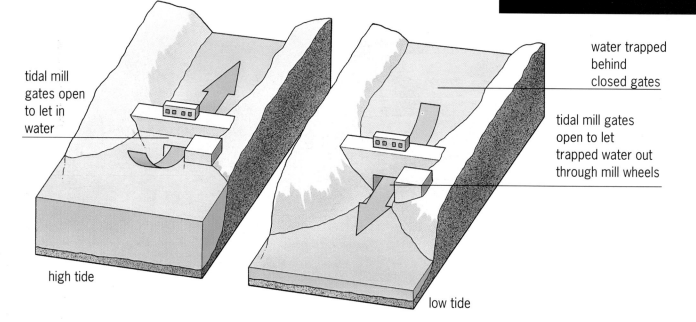

tidal mill gates open to let in water

high tide

water trapped behind closed gates

tidal mill gates open to let trapped water out through mill wheels

low tide

The disadvantage of tidal mills

Tidal mills could only be used for a few hours each day at low tide. And because the times of the tides changed each day, the miller's work hours had to change each day, too. In the twelfth century, tidal mills were built on the River Adour near Bayonne, France, and in the estuary of the River Deben in Suffolk, England. They grew in numbers right up to the nineteenth century, when about 100 tidal mills were working in Europe.

Inset photo opposite An illustration from *Physics in Pictures,* a science book published in 1882. It shows details of the mill wheels and gearing systems in both a windmill and water wheels.

Above: This tidal power barge anchored in the River Thames in England was used to operate wood working tools including a circular saw. A belt carried power from the 2-metre diameter wheel underneath the barge to the machinery on the deck.

Steam engines at work

Water power really came into its own with the development of the steam engine in the eighteenth century. When water turns to steam, it expands rapidly and with great force. One litre of water produces 1,300 litres of steam. This fact was known in ancient times. Hero of Alexandria made a steam-operated wheel called an aeolipile, but it was never more than an amusing toy. It was never used to do work. The French inventor Denis Papin was the first person to develop machines that used steam to do work, for example the pressure cooker. But history remembers Thomas Newcomen as the inventor of the first practical steam engine in 1712.

Left: A nineteenth-century diagram of a Watt steam engine. The new Watt engine was more efficient than Newcomen's and also very reliable.

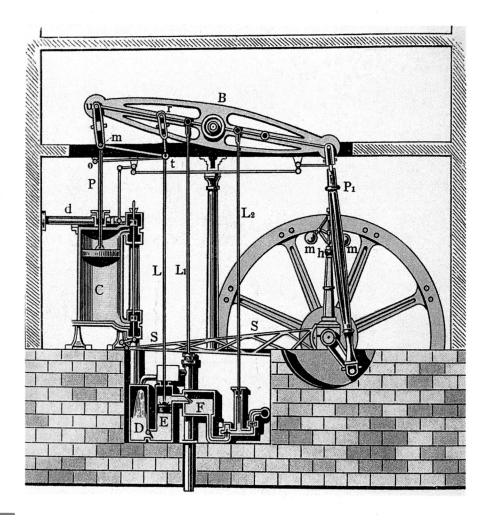

Right: Steam from a boiler forced into a piston can be used to turn a wheel, as this diagram shows.

FACTFILE

The first steam locomotive was built by Richard Trevithick in 1804. It pulled a load of ten tonnes and up to 70 people at a speed of 15km/h along a 15km-long track between an ironworks and canal in Wales.

A steam locomotive contains a water boiler heated by burning coal. Steam pressure from the boiler turns the wheels.

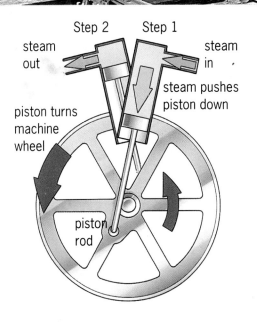

steam out

Step 2   Step 1

steam in

steam pushes piston down

piston turns machine wheel

piston rod

Steam-powered machines change the world

Newcomen's engine was designed to solve a particular problem. Deep mines often became flooded with water. Newcomen's steam engine was built to pump water out of mines. In 1765, James Watt improved Newcomen's design and used it to drive other types of machinery. By the end of the eighteenth century, hundreds of steam engines had been built. They rapidly transformed Britain, and then Europe and America, in a period that became known as the Industrial Revolution.

HARNESSING WATER POWER

An overshot water wheel like this is three times as efficient as an undershot wheel of the same size because the water's speed and weight both drive the wheel round.

FACTFILE

The idea for the water wheel probably came from ox-driven wheels used to raise water from rivers. As the wheel turned, pots or cups fixed to it filled up with water and then, as they rose and turned with the wheel, they emptied on to the riverbank. With the oxen unhitched, the wheel would have been turned by the flowing river.

Water-wheel technology

Water wheels were the first machines that made use of energy from moving water. No-one knows exactly where or when the first water wheels were made, but they were probably invented somewhere in the Middle East about 4,000 years ago.

Water wheels can be vertical or horizontal. Vertical wheels stand upright like a bicycle wheel. When the bottom of a vertical wheel is dipped in water, the force of the water pushing against paddles fixed round the edge pushes it round. This is called an undershot wheel because the water flows underneath it. Its speed depends on the speed of flow of the water.

An overshot vertical wheel turns faster because water runs on to it from above. The water's speed and weight both turn the wheel. The earliest known overshot wheel is shown on a wall-painting in the Roman catacombs made in the third century AD.

A horizontal water wheel lays flat. It is driven by water falling from above through a pipe or by a jet of water pointing at paddles or cups on the wheel rim.

Water wheels
There are two types of vertical water wheel – undershot and overshot – and a basic type of horizontal water wheel.

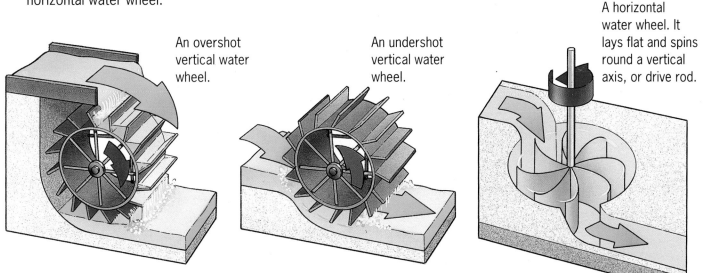

An overshot vertical water wheel.

An undershot vertical water wheel.

A horizontal water wheel. It lays flat and spins round a vertical axis, or drive rod.

Hydroelectric power

Moving water has energy that can do work. Hydro-electric power stations produce electricity from moving water. The water is guided into a turbine. When it hits the turbine's blades, the force of the water makes the turbine spin. The spinning turbine drives a generator, which converts movement energy into electrical energy.

Generators make more electricity if they spin faster. Turbine speed, and therefore the amount of electricity produced by the generator it drives, depends on water pressure. The greater the water pressure, the faster the turbine spins. Water pressure increases with depth.

At a typical hydroelectric power station, a deep lake called a reservoir is created by building a dam, or wall, across one end of a valley so that the valley fills up with water. Sluice gates can be opened to allow some of the water to escape so that the dam does not overflow. The water at the bottom of the reservoir is under great pressure because of the weight of water above it.

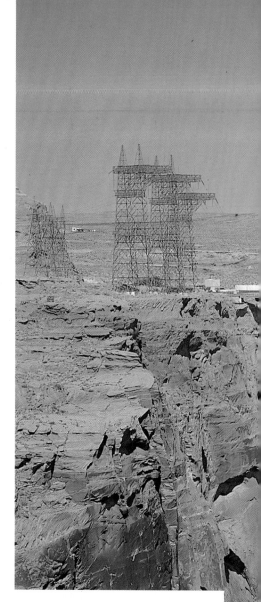

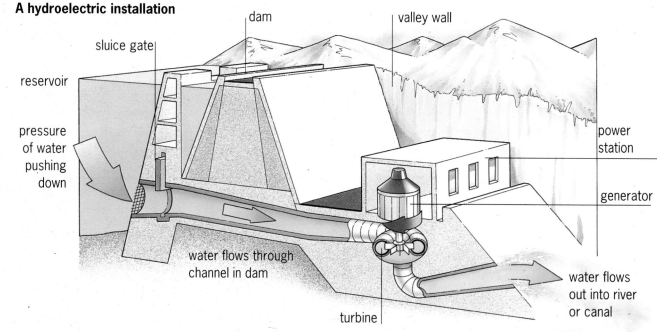

A hydroelectric installation

dam

valley wall

sluice gate

reservoir

pressure of water pushing down

power station

generator

water flows through channel in dam

water flows out into river or canal

turbine

The Glen Canyon Dam across the Colorado River in Arizona, USA, is part of a massive hydroelectric installation. It was completed in 1964. The reservoir behind it holds 40,000 million litres of water and stretches across the state border into Utah.

FACTFILE

Hydroelectric power stations provide one-fifth of the world's electricity. In developing countries, it provides more – up to 40 per cent of the electricity. Almost all the electricity used in Norway is produced by hydroelectric power stations. The world's most powerful power station is the Itaipu hydroelectric power plant on the Pirana River in South America. It generates 13,320 megawatts – enough electrical power for several cities.

Pumped storage power stations

The demand for electricity constantly changes throughout the day and night. It depends on the time, the day, the weather, and even the times of programmes on television! Power stations have to adjust their output to match these changing needs. One type of hydro-electric power station, called a pumped storage power station, uses spare electricity from other power stations when demand is low to store water that can be used to produce electricity when demand is high.

At night, when little electricity is needed, a pumped storage power station pumps water from a reservoir below it to a second reservoir above it. Then during the day, when more electricity is needed, the water is allowed to flow down to the lower reservoir through the power station's turbines. The turbines drive generators to produce electricity. When the demand for electricity falls again, the generators work in reverse as motors and drive the turbines. The turbines become pumps, which force the water back up to the higher reservoir, ready for the next day.

Opposite: The Ffestiniog complex. Pumped storage power stations need two reservoirs. At Ffestiniog in Wales, they were created by enlarging an existing reservoir and damming a river below the power station. If there is a sudden surge in demand for electricity, the generators here can produce 360 megawatts within 55 seconds – enough to supply thousands of homes.

The Vigario pumping station in Rio de Janeiro State, Brazil, pumps water uphill through pipes to its upper reservoir. The electricity it generates when it flows back through turbines is carried away by cables held high above the ground by towers called pylons.

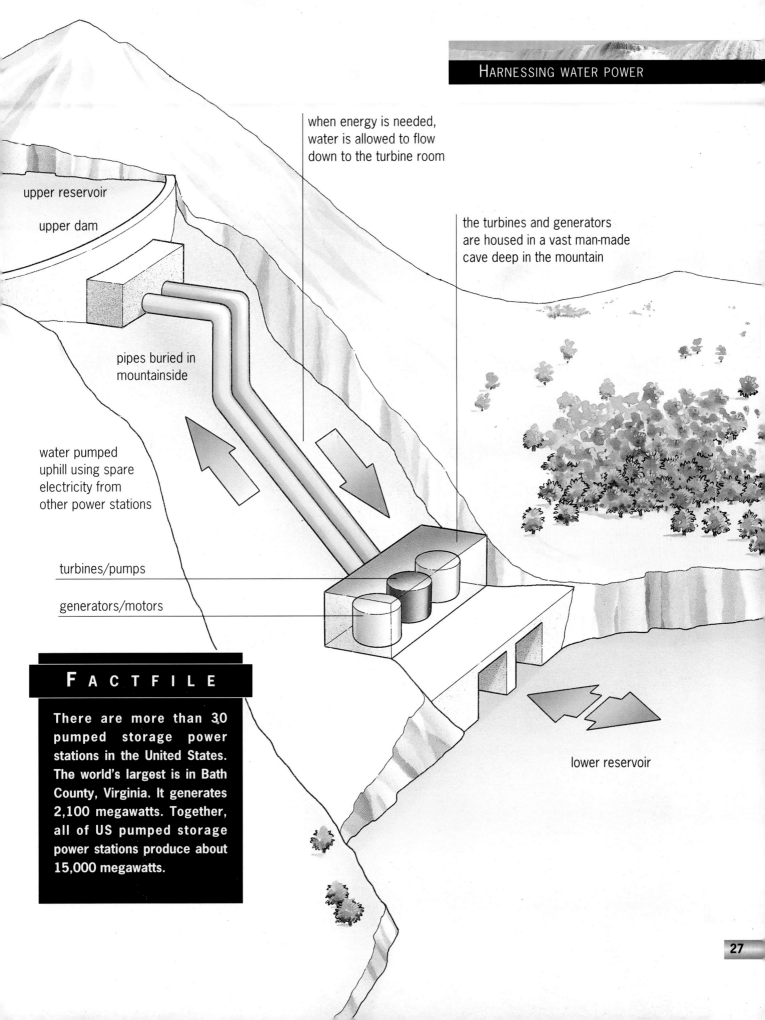

when energy is needed, water is allowed to flow down to the turbine room

the turbines and generators are housed in a vast man-made cave deep in the mountain

upper reservoir

upper dam

pipes buried in mountainside

water pumped uphill using spare electricity from other power stations

turbines/pumps

generators/motors

lower reservoir

FACTFILE

There are more than 30 pumped storage power stations in the United States. The world's largest is in Bath County, Virginia. It generates 2,100 megawatts. Together, all of US pumped storage power stations produce about 15,000 megawatts.

A dependence on hydroelectricity

Norwegians use more electricity than anyone else in the world. The demand for electricity in Norway has increased by more than half since 1975 and it continues to rise. At the beginning of the twentieth century, most of Norway's energy needs were met by burning wood and coal. Since then, electricity has gradually taken over. Norway could have built any type of power station, including fossil fuel and nuclear, to satisfy this demand, but the high mountains and heavy rainfall on its western coastline make Norway an ideal place to build hydroelectric power stations. More than 99 per cent of electricity in Norway is made from water in this way.

FACTFILE

Norwegians use about 30,000 kWh (kilowatt-hours) of electricity per person per year, the world's highest use of electricity This compares to about 6,000kWh per person in neighbouring Denmark and only 800kWh in Switzerland. Most of the electricity is used for heating and lighting.

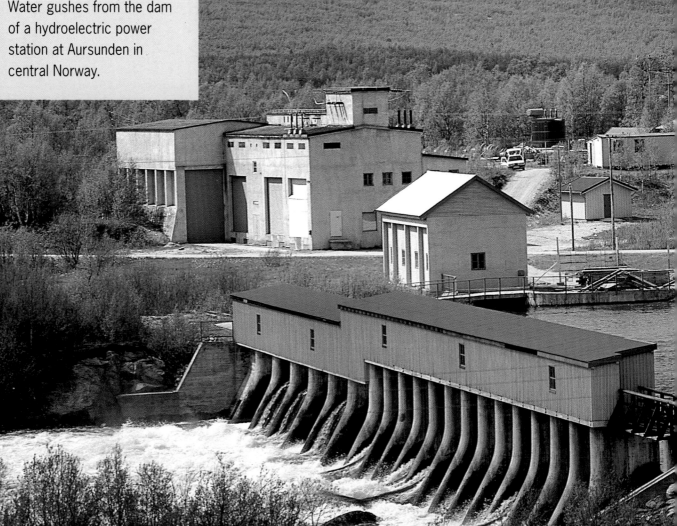

Water gushes from the dam of a hydroelectric power station at Aursunden in central Norway.

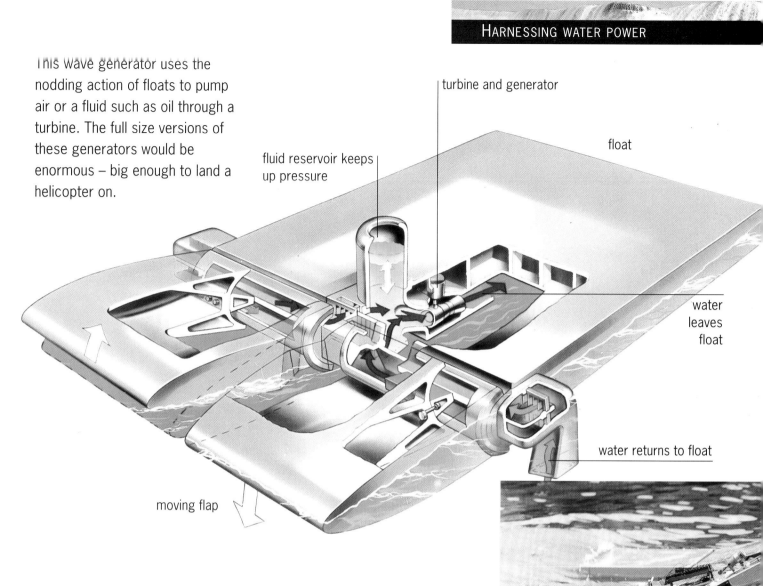

This wave generator uses the nodding action of floats to pump air or a fluid such as oil through a turbine. The full size versions of these generators would be enormous – big enough to land a helicopter on.

turbine and generator

float

fluid reservoir keeps up pressure

water leaves float

water returns to float

moving flap

Bobbing ducks and giant clams

Devices called Salter's Ducks, invented by Dr. Salter of Edinburgh University, Scotland, use the bobbing action of the waves to make electricity in this way. Another device called a clam works in a different way. A series of floating air bags are squeezed as passing waves rise and fall underneath them. Air inside the clam is squeezed from one bag to another. Generators between the bags spin as the air is pushed through. Both these devices are still experimental and small scale, and produce only small quantities of electricity.

Models of wave-energy generators are tested in a water tank before full-size versions are built. All the conditions in the tank are controlled so scientists can measure how good the generators are at using wave energy.

Oscillating water column generators

Waves rolling in towards the land from far out at sea push water against the coast with incredible power. This power can be harnessed in pipes or columns positioned along the coast. When water is pushed in through one end of a pipe, it forces air out of the other end. Oscillating water column generators use this effect to make electricity from waves. A chamber with an open top and bottom is set up on a cliff-face so that its bottom end is below the water surface.

This blow-hole in Australia was formed when water wore a tunnel through the rock. The force of each wave punches water through the funnel-shaped hole and blasts it out of the top. Oscillating water column generators harness the force of the sea in a similar way.

As waves rise and fall, the water level inside the chamber rises and falls too. When the water rises, it pushes air out of the top of the chamber. When the water falls again, it sucks air back in. If a turbine is fitted inside the chamber, the air rushing in and out of the chamber makes it spin. So, it is not the waves that generate electricity, it is the air above them.

A few experimental oscillating water column generators have been built. They were battered so badly by the constant pounding of the waves that most of them were destroyed. But research continues, and one day these power devices may contribute to our electricity needs.

Above: An oscillating water column generator on the coast of Norway.

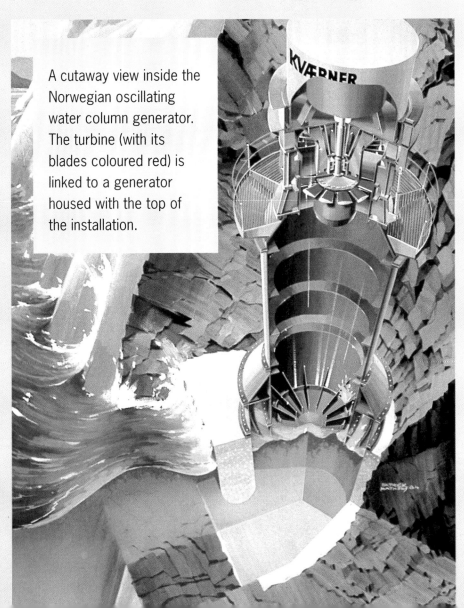

A cutaway view inside the Norwegian oscillating water column generator. The turbine (with its blades coloured red) is linked to a generator housed with the top of the installation.

Tidal barrages, or barriers

Huge quantities of water move with the tides each day. In some places the tide rushes in and out again fast enough to drive water turbines, but in most places the tides move too slowly. However, they can still be used to generate electricity by using exactly the same method that was used by medieval engineers to build tidal mills 800 years ago. The incoming tide is allowed to flow through sluice gates in a dam or barrage. At high tide, the gates are closed. As the tide ebbs and the water level outside the dam falls, the gates are opened to let the water rush out through turbines.

A threat to wildlife

Tidal power generators work for, at most, only ten hours a day. And the times when they can work keep changing with the tides. Another disadvantage is their effect on the environment. While they are pollution-free, they damage the environment in other ways. The river estuaries where tidal power stations are best built are often important feeding or breeding places for birds. The power stations are likely to drive the birds away.

The East Scheldt sea barrage in the Netherlands.

Birds like this curlew
sandpiper live and breed
on open ground and
shorelines in wet localities
such as estuaries. If power
stations are built in their
habitat, it may drive the
birds away.

A wall built across an estuary

The tidal barrage across the mouth of the River Rance at Saint-Malo in France was the first modern tidal power station of any size to be built. It is still the biggest tidal power station in the world. Since it was opened in 1966, it has been generating a constant flow of about 240 megawatts of electricity – enough to supply a quarter of a million homes. The river and the open sea are separated by a wall 750 metres long. Water can pass through it by means of 24 tunnels. Each tunnel contains a turbine and a generator.

FACTFILE

The River Rance reaches the sea in the bay of Saint-Malo in north-west France where the Channel meets the Atlantic Ocean. Here the difference in height between high and low tide can reach

Cutaway view of the tidal barrage at La Rance

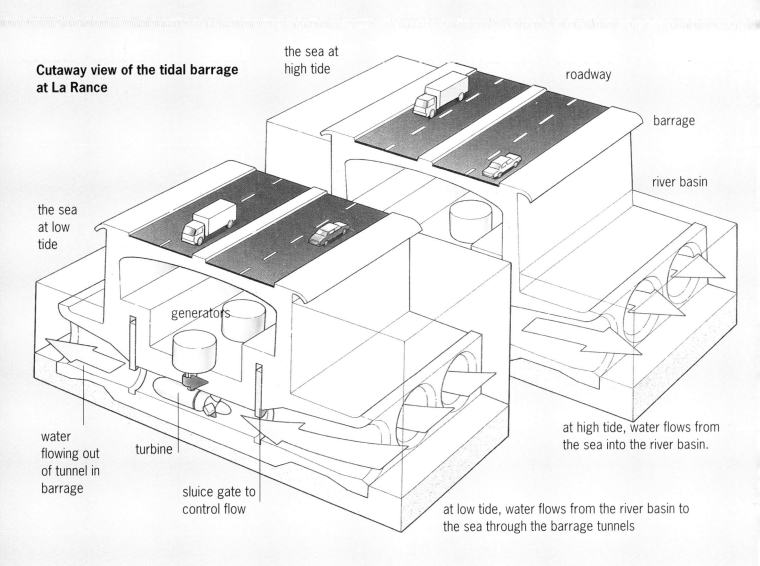

the sea at high tide

roadway

barrage

river basin

the sea at low tide

generators

water flowing out of tunnel in barrage

turbine

sluice gate to control flow

at high tide, water flows from the sea into the river basin.

at low tide, water flows from the river basin to the sea through the barrage tunnels

The tidal barrage at La Rance stretches across the river-mouth between Saint-Malo and Dinard. The roadway across the barrage reduces the distance of the journey between the two towns by car by 15 kilometres.

The Gulf of Saint-Malo catches tides flowing in from the Atlantic and funnels them into the mouth of the River Rance, squeezing the water into the narrowing channel and speeding it up. The result is that the tides on the Rance are powerful enough to drive the turbines on both the incoming and outgoing tides.

Most turbines are designed to work with water or steam travelling in one direction only, but the turbines built into the Rance tidal barrage function just as well in whichever direction the water flows. With the tide in full flood, each generator produces up to 10 megawatts of electricity.

PUTTING WATER POWER TO WORK

Steam turbines

Water wheels are still in use today, but the real power behind water-driven machinery today is the steam turbine. When water is heated and changed into steam, the steam expands outwards at an enormous speed and with great force. This expansion can be put to work.

A steam engine produces an up-down or back-and-forth motion of a piston which has to be changed into a spinning motion to drive machines. Steam turbines are much simpler. They produce a spinning motion straight away, doing away with all the complicated mechanical linkages that go with a steam engine. Unlike water wheels, which are usually open to the weather, steam turbines must be sealed inside an air-tight case so that the high-pressure steam cannot leak out.

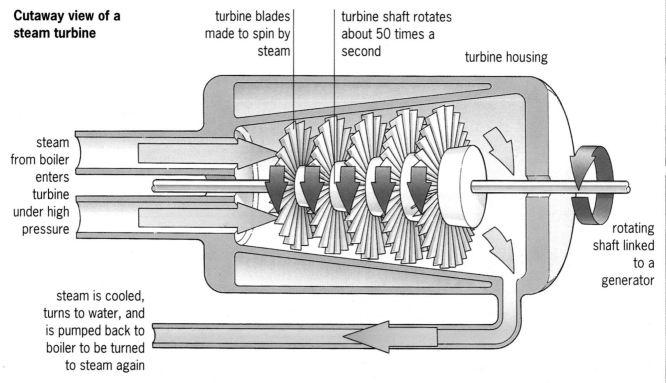

Cutaway view of a steam turbine

turbine blades made to spin by steam

turbine shaft rotates about 50 times a second

turbine housing

steam from boiler enters turbine under high pressure

rotating shaft linked to a generator

steam is cooled, turns to water, and is pumped back to boiler to be turned to steam again

In the simplest of steam turbines, the speed of steam pushing against the turbine blades makes the drive shaft rotate. In other steam turbines there is an extra set of blades, which are fixed in position. As the steam, still expanding, passes through the fixed blades, it speeds up before hitting the moving blades. This turns the drive shaft harder and faster.

Inside the steam turbine and generator room of a nuclear power station. Here, the steam pipes are coloured silver and the pairs of turbines and generators are coloured red, blue and yellow.

The Boeing Jetfoil is a water-jet powered hydrofoil. As it speeds up, underwater wings lift its hull out of the water. The engines suck water in through the rear wing and pump it out through the stern.

Water-jet engines

Most ships and boats are powered by engines driving propellers, which are blades fixed to a central rod that is turned at high speed. Propellers can be damaged if they hit the seabed in shallow water or they can get tangled up in weeds or ropes. Propellers are also very dangerous if there are people in the water nearby.

A different type of engine, called a water-jet engine, suffers from none of these disadvantages. Instead of spinning a propeller, the engine pumps out a high-speed jet of water. A large volume of water is sucked in through the bottom of the craft, speeded up by pumps and concentrated into a much narrower and faster jet.

High-speed sea craft

The same water jet can also be used to steer the craft, by swivelling the jet to one side or the other. The world's fastest and largest car ferries are powered by water-jet engines. They use the same jet engines as fighter-planes and airliners. Instead of producing a jet of air, they drive pumps that move amazing amounts of water. When the HSS 1500 car ferry's engines are running at full power, they pump out 85,000 litres (about 250 bathfuls) of water every second!

An ocean-going ferry such as a SeaCat sucks in water through the bottom of the craft and pumps water out through steering water jets at the back. The craft can reach speeds of 42 knots (about 76km/hr.)

A water-bike skims across shallow water using its water-jet engines.

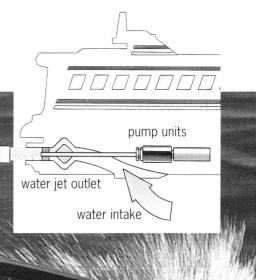

pump units

water jet outlet

water intake

Kawasaki

FACTFILE

Jets of water from hoses have been used to wash out ore-bearing gravels and sands for decades. However, cutting materials like metal and wood by means of a water jet is a much more recent development. This type of

Water-jet tools

Water in nature can carve caves out of rock, bring down cliffs and wash away roads and bridges. Water jets are sometimes used in a similar way in mining, to cut through earth containing valuable minerals and wash it down into a collection area. China clay is extracted in this way. More powerful water jets cut through coal.

When water is concentrated into a thin jet, it can cut through tough materials in a highly controlled way. A high-pressure jet of water can clean something by blasting off the dirt. The black crust of grime caused by years of air pollution is stripped off stone buildings in this way. If the pressure is boosted still further, it can cut through the material itself, not just dirt on its surface. The most advanced water cutting tools work at water pressures of sufficient to break reinforced concrete. Harsh rocky particles are added to the water to improve its cutting power. Water-jet tools can now drill or cut through such materials as steel and titanium.

A compressor is used to pump water to a nozzle, which sprays it out as a jet of dirt-removing droplets.

THE FUTURE OF WATER POWER

Harnessing the heat of oceans

Tidal power and wave power are at an early stage in their development. But as fossil fuels begin to run out, we are likely to build more tidal barrages across river estuaries and more wave-power generators along coasts. There may also be machines called OTECs (Ocean Thermal Energy Converters) making electricity in warm tropical seas. Ocean temperature falls with depth. The surface may be as warm as 25 °C, while deeper water is nearly freezing. This difference in temperature is used to evaporate a liquid and so drive a turbine.

In an OTEC machine, warm surface water evaporates a liquid such as ammonia. The vapour drives a turbine and is then changed back to a liquid by cold water pumped up from the depths.

crew quarters with helipad on the roof

warm water intake

warm surface water

warm water outlet

turbine

condenser

cold water outlet

intake pipe: 30 metres in diameter and up to 1,000 metres long

cold deep water

cold water riser pipe

anchorage cable

A handful of small experimental OTECs have been built, but so far no large commercial OTEC machines have been constructed.

Power generators in the sea have to withstand constant pounding from waves and tides. Plants and animals that make their home on and inside any machine in seawater could damage it or make it less effective. But as all renewable energy sources are investigated more in future, these problems will eventually be overcome. In the meantime, conventional hydroelectric schemes and low-technology, inexpensive water mills will continue to be built.

Controllers in a future power station look out over rows of wave power generators. Their computers monitor the sea conditions and the power output of the generators.

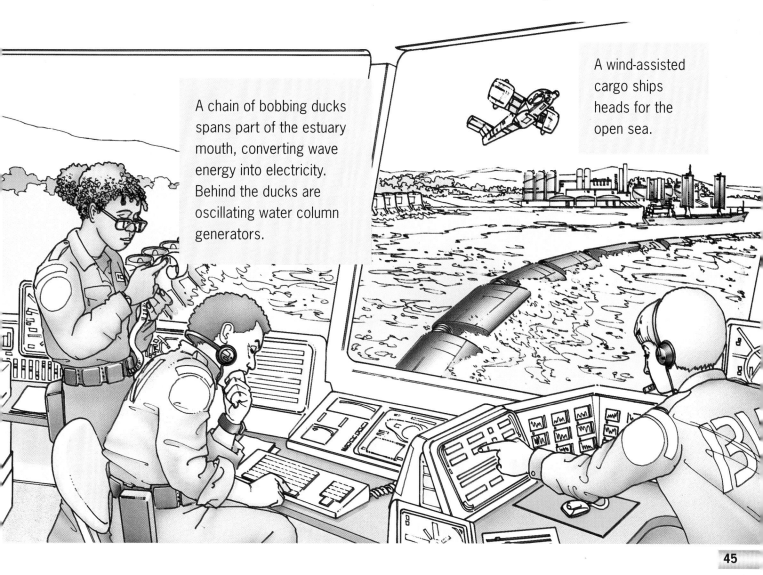

A chain of bobbing ducks spans part of the estuary mouth, converting wave energy into electricity. Behind the ducks are oscillating water column generators.

A wind-assisted cargo ships heads for the open sea.

GLOSSARY

Atmosphere The gases that surround the Earth, containing mostly nitrogen (78 per cent) and oxygen (21 per cent).

Atom The smallest particle of matter that can take part in chemical reactions.

Billion One thousand million.

Boiler A water tank designed for heating water and turning it into steam.

Carbon dioxide A gas containing carbon and oxygen that forms 0.03 per cent of the Earth's atmosphere.

Clam A shellfish and also the name of a type of wave power generator.

Dam A barrier built to hold back water.

Dyke A land barrier built to stop the sea from flooding low-lying land, especially in the Netherlands.

Estuary The tidal mouth of a river where it meets the sea.

Evaporate Change from a liquid into a gas.

Fossil fuel Coal, oil and natural gas – fuels formed in prehistoric times from the decay of plants and microscopic animals.

Generator A machine designed to change movement energy into electrical energy.

Glacier A large mass of ice on land formed from snow. The deepest layers of snow are compressed (squeezed) by the weight of snow above them and change into hard glacier ice.

Global warming An increase in the Earth's temperature that may be happening because of human activities.

Great Ocean Conveyor Belt The main ocean current that drives seawater around the world.

Horizon The line where the Earth and the sky seem to meet.

Hurricane A violent circular storm that forms over water in the Atlantic Ocean, especially in the Caribbean Sea.

Hydroelectric power Electricity generated by the energy of falling water.

Hydrofoil A type of boat with underwater wings that lift its hull out of the water when it accelerates.

Hydrogen The lightest and most common of all gases in the Universe.

Kilo- The first part of a word meaning 1,000 as in kilowatt, kilometre.

Kilowatt A unit of electrical power meaning 1,000 watts.

Kilowatt-hour A unit of electrical energy equivalent to 1,000 watts used for one hour.

Mega- The first part of a word meaning one million.

Megawatt A unit of electrical power meaning one million watts – enough to supply the total needs of a family house.

Monsoon A seasonal wind over India and south Asia blowing from the south-west in summer and from the north-east in winter.

Neap tide A small tide that occurs at the Moon's first and third quarters.

Oscillating wave column generator A type of electricity generator that changes the up-down motion of sea waves into electricity.

OTEC Ocean Thermal Energy Converter. A machine for making electricity by using the difference in temperature between water at different depths.

Overshot A type of water wheel powered by water falling on it from above.

Piston The part of an engine that slides up and down inside a close-fitting cylinder.

Reservoir A large natural or artificial lake used as a supply of water.

Salter's Duck A wave power generator that produces electricity from the bobbing action of waves.

Sluice gate A gate fitted to a water channel to control the amount of water passing through it.

Spring tide A high tide that occurs at the New Moon or Full Moon when the Sun, Moon and Earth are in line.

Steam engine An engine powered by steam pressure.

Tidal power station A power station that generates electricity by using the tides.

Tidal range The difference in sea level between high and low tides.

Tide The daily rise and fall in sea level caused by the gravitational pull of the Moon and Sun.

Tsunami A large, powerful and destructive wave caused by an underwater earthquake.

Turbine A machine that uses a moving fluid such as water or oil, or a vapour like steam, to spin a wheel or drum with blades set around its edge.

Typhoon A violent storm in the Pacific Ocean.

Undershot A type of water wheel driven by water flowing underneath it.

Water cycle The circulation of water from land and sea to the atmosphere and back to the land and sea again.

Water jet engine A type of engine that propels a ship or water-bike by means of a high-pressure jet of water.

Water mill A grain mill in which the mill stone is driven by a water wheel.

Water wheel A wheel driven by running water.

Books to read

Acid Rain by Alex Edmonds (Franklin Watts, 1996)

Alternative Energy: Water Energy by Graham Rickard (Wayland, 1990)

Designs in Science: Water by Sally and Adrian Morgan (Evans Brothers, 1994)

Eyewitness Science: Energy by Jack Challoner (Dorling Kindersley and London Science Museum, 1993)

Fusion: The Search for Endless Energy by Robert Herman (CUP, 1990)

Renewable Energy: Sources for Fuels and Electricity by T.B Johansson and others (Island Press, 1993)

Science Works: Energy by Steve Parker (Macdonald Young Books, 1995)

Power and energy consumption

Power is the measurement of how quickly energy is used. It is measured in joules per second, or watts. An electric iron might need 1,000 watts to work, but a portable radio might need only 10 watts. The energy needed to keep the radio going for one hour would run the iron for only six minutes, because the iron uses up energy ten times faster than the radio. The diagram to the right compares the power ratings of household electrical goods and of homes and power stations.

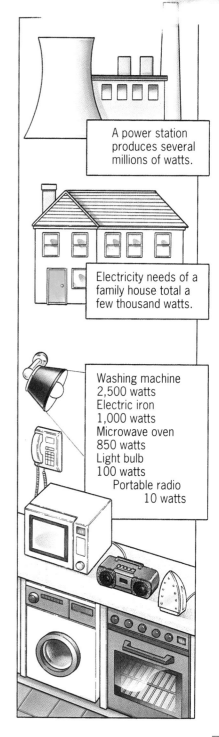

A power station produces several millions of watts.

Electricity needs of a family house total a few thousand watts.

Washing machine 2,500 watts
Electric iron 1,000 watts
Microwave oven 850 watts
Light bulb 100 watts
Portable radio 10 watts

INDEX